YOUR KNOWLEDGE HAS VALUE

Uqbah Iqbal

Japanese Economic Interests in Sabah after the Second World War

GRIN Publishing

Bibliographic information published by the German National Library:

The German National Library lists this publication in the National Bibliography; detailed bibliographic data are available on the Internet at http://dnb.dnb.de .

Imprint:

Copyright © 2015 GRIN Verlag GmbH
Print and binding: Books on Demand GmbH, Norderstedt Germany
ISBN: 978-3-656-96933-4

This book at GRIN:

http://www.grin.com/en/e-book/298463/japanese-economic-interests-in-sabah-after-the-second-world-war

GRIN - Your knowledge has value

Since its foundation in 1998, GRIN has specialized in publishing academic texts by students, college teachers and other academics as e-book and printed book. The website www.grin.com is an ideal platform for presenting term papers, final papers, scientific essays, dissertations and specialist books.

Visit us on the internet:

http://www.grin.com/

http://www.facebook.com/grincom

http://www.twitter.com/grin_com

JAPANESE ECONOMIC INTERESTS IN SABAH AFTER THE SECOND WORLD WAR

Abstract

The development of the Malaysian economy currently inherited from three previous levels, starting from the growth and rapid development level of natural resources industries from the mid 19th century until the year 1914, followed by a volatility or instability period of natural resources industries between the First and Second World War and last but not least the level of consolidation and rationalisation of natural resources industries together with a diversified economy after 1945. Although Malaysia is a former British colony, the importance of Japan's economy has contributed to the change of the foreign policy from the Pro-West Policy during the colonial and post-colonial era to the Look-to-The-East Policy during the administration of Tun Dr. Mahathir Mohamad. Therefore the main issue of this study is to unravel the importance of Japanese economic in North Borneo and Sabah after the Second World War. In terms of the methodology used, this research entails identifying and collecting primary and secondary sources from the library, the National Archives of Malaysia and National Library of Singapore.

Keywords: Economic, Japan, North Borneo, Sabah

Introduction

The economic importance of Japan in North Borneo before the Second World War was touched in passing by several writers. Among the studies that seen as crucial is Yutaka Shimomoto in the book *Japanese Immigrants and Investments in North Borneo*,[1] Sabihah Osman in the article *Japanese Economic Activities in Sabah from the 1890s until 1941*,[2] Md. Saffie Abdul Rahim in the book *Jepun di Borneo Utara: Migrasi dan Kegiatan Ekonomi*

---

[1] Yutaka Shimomoto & Mandalam, K. Ravi (editors), *Japanese Immigrants and Investments in North Borneo*, Kota Kinabalu, The Sabah Society, 2010.

[2] Sabihah Osman, Japanese economic activities in North Borneo from the 1890s until 1941 in *Journal of Southeast Asian Studies* 29 (1), 1998, pp. 24-43.

1884-1941[3] and Md. Saffie bin Abdul Rahim in thesis *Sejarah Kegiatan Ekonomi Orang Jepun di Borneo Utara sebelum Perang Dunia Kedua (1890-1941)*.[4] Japanese economic interests in North Borneo after independence, followed by the formation of Malaysia after it has been touched by many previous researchers, among the most important research are from Chee Peng Lim & Lee Poh Ping in the book *The Role of Japanese Direct Investment in Malaysia*[5] and in chapter *Japanese Direct Investment in Malaysia, with Special Reference to Japanese Joint Ventures*,[6] Mehmet Sami Denker in thesis *Internationalization of the Malaysian Economy: Role of Japan*[7] and chapter *The Evolution of Japanese Investment in Malaysia*,[8] Makoto Anazawa in chapter *Japanese Manufacturing Investment in Malaysia*[9] and Md. Ali Hasan in paper *Pelaburan Langsung Jepun di Malaysia*.[10] All of these resources help in the form of research. The difference with this study is that the researcher will use resources that are different from all previous studies.

Malaya, North Borneo and Sarawak were allocated by 5,004,000 pound sterling for direct import from Japan under the trade agreement between the Sterling Area and the occupation of Japan by the Supreme Commander of the Allied Powers (SCAP) from dari 1 July

---

[3] Md. Saffie Abdul Rahim, *Jepun di Borneo Utara: Migrasi dan Kegiatan Ekonomi 1884-1941*, Kota Kinabalu, Penerbit UMS, 2007.

[4] Md. Saffie bin Abdul Rahim, *Sejarah Kegiatan Ekonomi Orang Jepun di Borneo Utara sebelum Perang Dunia Kedua (1890-1941)*, Master's Thesis in Literature, Sekolah Sains Sosial, Universiti Malaysia Sabah, 2005.

[5] Chee Peng Lim & Lee Poh Ping, *The Role of Japanese Direct Investment in Malaysia*, Occasional Paper No. 60, Singapore, Institute of Southeast Asian Studies, 1979.

[6] Chee Peng Lim & Lee Poh Ping, Japanese Direct Investment in Malaysia, with Special Reference to Japanese Joint Ventures in Sueo Sekiguchi (editor), *ASEAN-Japan Relations Investment*, Singapore, Institute of Southeast Asian Studies, 1983, pp. 61-92.

[7] Mehmet Sami Denker, *Internationalization of the Malaysian Economy: Role of Japan*, Ph.D. Thesis, Universiti Malaya, 1990.

[8] Mehmet Sami Denker, The Evolution of Japanese Investment in Malaysia in Jomo, K.S. (editor), *Japan and Malaysian Development: In the shadow of the rising sun*, London, Routledge, 1994, pp. 44-74.

[9] Makoto Anazawa, Japanese Manufacturing Investment in Malaysia in Jomo, K.S. (editor), *Japan and Malaysian Development: In the shadow of the rising sun*, London, Routledge, 1994, pp. 75-101.

[10] Md. Ali Hasan, *Pelaburan Langsung Jepun di* Malaysia, Kertas kerja Kongres Sejarah Malaysia II - Sejarah dan Proses Pemantapan Negara Bangsa, Anjuran Persatuan Sejarah Malaysia dengan kerjasama Jabatan Sejarah UKM, Bilik Jumaah UKM, Bangi, 26-28 November 1996.

1949 until 30 June 1950.[11] There are also Anglo-Japanese joint plans for 20 years to exploit timber and other resources such as Manila hemp, rubber, coffee and cocoa in North Borneo. Although Japan plays an important role in assisting the development of Southeast Asia, it must address the sentiments of local residents due to the Second World War.[12] On 8 April 1957, the Consul General of Japan in Singapore, Ken Ninomiya states Japan willing to provide technical assistance to North Borneo to help its development under the Colombo Plan, especially in agriculture and fisheries. North Borneo Government can choose whether to accept the arrival of Japanese technicians or send young people who are able to research and training in Japan. There are possibilities for joint ventures in commercial and Japan is willing to cooperate.[13] On 30 March 1957, Consul General of Japan in Singapore, Ken Ninomiya stated the possibility of increasing the number of direct trade between Japan and North Borneo were discussed with the government of North Borneo. Japan is the largest customer of North Borneo for wood and sells construction materials in return.[14] From 1959 to 1962 under the Colombo Plan, the Japanese government has received a total of seven trainees of North Borneo and sent a total of 13 experts to Singapore, North Borneo and Sarawak.[15]

On 4 October 1964, the Chief Minister of Sabah, Dato' Donald Stephens declared Japan have shown keen interest to invest in Sabah development projects. Japan is keen to establish joint ventures with local entrepreneurs, especially in the plywood industry, but it is hampered by labor problems. He thanked the Peninsular Malaysia as trying to solve the labor shortage problem in Sabah. Workers in Peninsular Malaysia should be given a true picture because most of them are of the opinion that Sabah is unsafe. These things are not true because Sabah is the safest place to work.[16] On 29 November 1966, the Chief Minister of Sabah, Peter Lo

---

[11] Anonymous, 5 MILLION IMPORTS FROM JAPAN in *The Straits Times*, 16 November 1949, p. 1. See also Anonymous, $1mil. Import From Japan in *The Straits Times*, 31 March 1950, p. 4.

[12] Anonymous, Japs want to develop North Borneo in *The Singapore Free Press*, 23 July 1952, p. 3. See also Anonymous, Awards May Be Paid This Year. NORTH BORNEO WAR DAMAGE in *The Straits Times*, 28 April 1950, p. 4.

[13] Anonymous, Japan pledges support for North Borneo. OFFER TO HELP AGRICULTURE, FISHERIES... in *The Straits Times*, 9 April 1957, p. 12.

[14] Anonymous, Trade boost plan in *The Straits Times*, 31 March 1957, p. 11.

[15] Anonymous, Japan's technical co-operation in *The Straits Times*, 15 September 1963, p. 7.

[16] Anonymous, JAPANESE INTEREST IN SABAH PROJECTS in *The Straits Times*, 5 October 1964, p. 11.

said that there was interest from Japanese entrepreneurs to invest in Sabah. They are interested in agricultural development and exploitation of Sabah mineral resources. Japanese entrepreneurs that come here should arrange a joint venture with local capital.[17]

In October 1959, Japan imported a total of 700 tons of raw rubber from North Borneo.[18] In November 1959, Japan imported a total of 170 tons of natural rubber from North Borneo.[19] By 1961, 20 percent or North Borneo highest total imports came from Britain, while the highest export volume of 43.38 percent went to Japan.[20] In 1962, imports from Japan to North Borneo totaled $18.4 million, while exports to Japan from North Borneo totaled $116.2 million. North Borneo wood exports to Japan in that year totaled $91 million or 75 percent from the total exports of North Borneo's timber. Japan also bought copra valued at $12.6 million from North Borneo in 1962.[21] Japan began to establish a consulate in Kota Kinabalu in 1965. Apart from sending volunteers overseas to help advance the agriculture and fisheries industries in Sabah, Japan also offers an estimated 100 scholarships per year to young people of Sabah.[22] There is also the first Pisang Embun exports from Sabah to Japan by 30 tons in May 1970.[23]

Japanese interest in Sabah economic development after the formation of Malaysia can be seen through donations, official visits, economic visits and social visits from Japan from time to time, among them are Governor of Kagawa-Ken Prefecture visit, Masanori on 23 May 23 1964,[24] offer of scholarships for one Sabah youth in social sciences and humanities and the

---

[17] Anonymous, Lo: Japanese keen to invest in Sabah in *The Straits Times*, 29 November 1966, p. 13.

[18] Anonymous, JAPAN'S RUBBER IMPORTS FALL OFF in *The Straits Times*, 1 January 1960, p. 12.

[19] Anonymous, Japan rubber imports up in *The Straits Times*, 12 January 1960, p. 10.

[20] Anonymous, North Borneo bid for investment cash from abroad. NEEDED TO HELP SPEED THE TERRITORY'S TRADE AND INDUSTRIAL DEVELOPMENT in *The Straits Times*, 1 December 1961, p. 13.

[21] Anonymous, Borneo timber is one of territories' big exports to Japan. TRADE WITH BORNEO in *The Straits Times*, 15 September 1963, p. 1.

[22] James Chia, Sabah: Jepun meluaskan rancangan ekonomi-nya in *Berita Harian*, 16 September 1968, p. 3. See also Anonymous, Japs want to develop North Borneo in *The Singapore Free Press*, 23 July 1952, p. 3.

[23] Anonymous, Sabah bananas for Japan in *The Straits Times*, 11 May 1970, p. 6.

[24] Anonymous, New fishing firm in Sandakan in *The Straits Times*, 24 May 1964, p. 10.

natural sciences postgraduate studies in 1965,[25] offers from a Japanese company to train 50 youths from Sabah, Sarawak and Brunei for free in Japan in the course of making furniture for three years on 22 March 1967,[26] Monbusho Scholarship program deals from the Japanese government for a graduate student and a pre-degree student majoring in Arts to study at Japanese universities in 1967,[27] Overseas Mineral Resources Company granted permission to mine Mamut copper area located at Mount Kinabalu in 1967,[28] the arrival of Japanese observers to see the Sabah election on 4 April 1967,[29] the arrival of four Japanese volunteers on 12 December 1968,[30] the Prime Minister, Tunku Abdul Rahman received donations of $200,000 from the Sabah government on 8 August 1969 to assist Malaysia in EXPO 1970 participation to be held in Osaka, Japan,[31] Nippon Koei Company Limited signed a contract on 8 September 1978 with Sabah Electricity Board to oversee the Tenom Pangi hydroelectric project near the Sarawak border,[32] Sabah Electricity Board signed a contract with Tobishima Maeda, a Japanese joint venture company for civil works for hydro-electric power station worth $250 million on 1 March 1979,[33] Sabah government's decision to establish a representative office timber along the Indonesian government in Tokyo on 30 May 1979,[34] Sabah government's plan on 3 November 1981 to choose Japan as a foreign partner in

---

[25] Anonymous, JAPANESE AWARDS FOR SABAH, SARAWAK in *The Straits Times*, 11 December 1964, p. 11. See also Anonymous, Japan offers five scholarships in *The Straits Times*, 4 April 1964, p. 6.

[26] Albert Ramalingam, Firm offers 50 youths training with pay in Japan in *The Straits Times*, 22 March 1967, p. 6.

[27] Anonymous, Tokyo offers Sabah two scholarships in *The Straits Times*, 25 September 1966, p. 14.

[28] Anonymous, Sharikat Jepun di-beri hak korek tembaga. Bakal lombong paling besar di-Malaysia in *Berita Harian*, 17 November 1967, p. 1. See also Anonymous, Minyak di-Sabah. 'Kemungkinan baik': Empat sharikat asing di-beri lesen in *Berita Harian*, 28 December 1965, p. 1. See also Anonymous, Jepun mula buat jalan menuju lombong tembaga in *Berita Harian*, 28 December 1967, p. 3. See also Anonymous, Sharikat2 chari emas dan Perak di-Sabah in *Berita Harian*, 12 May 1970, p. 3. See also Anonymous, Japan gets license to prospect in *The Straits Times*, 10 December 1967, p. 11.

[29] Anonymous, 6 NEGARA AKAN MELIHAT P-RAYA SABAH in *Berita Harian*, 22 March 1967, p. 1.

[30] Anonymous, Sukarelawan Jepun in *Berita Harian*, 8 December 1968, p. 12.

[31] Anonymous, $200,000 untok Expo dari Sabah in *Berita Harian*, 7 August 1969, p. 1.

[32] Anonymous, Nippon Koei to oversee Sabah power project in *The Business Times*, 9 September 1978, p. 2.

[33] Anonymous, Hydro-power contract in *The Straits Times*, 1 March 1979, p. 13.

[34] Anonymous, Joint timber office in Tokyo in *The Business Times*, 31 May 1979, p. 3.

establishing a factory producing cocoa-based products,[35] Chief Minister of Sabah prompt, Datuk Harris Salleh on 10 February 1982 for Japan offers technical assistance and loans to Sabah to renew and preserve the country's timber resources dwindling,[36] Marubeni Corporation joint venture in Sabah to process veneer board in Sandakan in June 1982,[37] the giving of Taman Damai Labuan worth $2 million and measuring 4.5 hectares from various Japanese organizations in April 1984,[38] a contribution of $15 thousand from the Prince and Princess Hitachi and members of the Japanese community in Sabah on 8 June 8 1984 for Orang Utan Rehabilitation Centre in Sepilok, Sandakan,[39] filming made by a Japanese television staff team about the Murut community in Sabah in June 1988,[40] Prime Minister prompting, Dato' Seri Dr. Mahathir Mohamad on 27 July 1994 for Japanese investors to put their industry in the Eastern Corridor of Peninsular Malaysia, Sabah and Sarawak to help accelerate the development of these areas.[41]

There are also visit from the Japanese Consul, T. J. Nakagawa on 4 April 1894,[42] visit from the representative of Southern Emigrating Association of Kobe, M. Inouye on 30 November 1894,[43] visit from the study group consisted of 11 people from Japan Federation of Economic Management Organisation in May 1959,[44] visit from 11 Japanese businessmen at the end of May 1959,[45] visit from the Consul General of Japan in Singapore, Kenseku Maeda

---

[35] Anonymous, Sabah cocoa venture in *The Straits Times*, 4 November 1981, p. 19.

[36] Anonymous, JAPAN IS URGED TO OFFER HELP TO SABAH in *The Straits Times*, 10 February 1982, p. 13.

[37] Anonymous, Marubeni in Sabah veneer venture in *The Business Times*, 8 July 1981, p. 2.

[38] Anonymous, Sabah gets $2 m 'peace garden' from Japan in *The Straits Times*, 17 April 1984, p. 15.

[39] Anonymous, Japanese gift of $15,000 to ape centre in *The Straits Times*, 9 June 1984, p. 20.

[40] Anonymous, Menlu belum lihat filem in *Berita Harian*, 20 June 1988, p. 2.

[41] Anonymous, Invest in east coast, Sabah and Sarawak: Mahathir in *The Straits Times*, 28 July 1994, p. 15.

[42] Anonymous, JAPANESE IMMIGRATION IN BRITISH NORTH BORNEO. in *The Straits Times*, 31 May 1894, p. 24.

[43] Anonymous, JAPANESE IN BRITISH NORTH BORNEO. in *The Straits Times*, 21 January 1895, p. 3.

[44] Anonymous, Japanese industry team for Borneo in *The Straits Times*, 18 April 1959, p. 2.

[45] Anonymous, Jepun na' lawat Borneo Utara in *Berita Harian*, 2 May 1959, p. 3.

and Vice Consul, Sadao Saito in March 1961,[46] visit from the Consul General of Japan in Singapore, T. Ueda in May 1964,[47] Japan's trade mission visit about 7 people in May 1964,[48] the arrival of 4 volunteers from Japan Overseas Corporation in December 1965,[49] the arrival of two Japanese Foreign Ministry officials as observers in Sabah Legislative Council elections on 8 April 1967,[50] the arrival of 10 volunteers from Japan Overseas Cooperation on 7 April 1970.[51]

There is also the entry of Japanese investments from time to time, such as the opening of the North Borneo Fishing Company Limited on 25 May 1964,[52] Teiseki Sabah Oil Company obtained permission to conduct the search for oil exploration on an area of 7,500 square miles in Sabah East Coast sea in February 1969,[53] Sumitomo Group and Teikoku Oil Company signed a letter of agreement with the Aquitaine Petroleum Company on 8 May 8 1969 to explore and develop the French company offshore concession in the North East Sabah,[54] Japanese Overseas Mineral Resources Development Co. plan in May 1969 to invest a total of approximately US $50 million in projects to exploit the copper mines in Mamut,[55] the first

---

[46] Anonymous, Diplomats tour N. Borneo in *The Straits Times*, 8 March 1961, p. 16.

[47] Anonymous, Japan to have man in Borneo in *The Straits Times*, 15 May 1964, p. 8.

[48] Anonymous, Japan keen to take part in Sabah development in *The Straits Times*, 30 May 1964, p. 9.

[49] Anonymous, 7 Japanese peace corps volunteers due in *The Straits Times*, 24 December 1965, p. 11.

[50] Anonymous, JEPUN KIRIM PEMERHATI2 KA-PILEHAN RAYA SABAH in *Berita Harian*, 31 March 1967, p. 3.

[51] Anonymous, 10 volunteers from Japan in *The Straits Times*, 7 April 1970, p. 15.

[52] Anonymous, New fishing firm in Sandakan in *The Straits Times*, 24 May 1964, p. 10.

[53] Anonymous, Sharikat dari Jepun di-berikan tugas. BERJUTA2 UNTOK MENCHARI MINYAK in *Berita Harian*, 4 February 1969, p. 2. See also Anonymous, JAPANESE TO DRILL OIL WELLS IN BORNEO in *The Straits Times*, 5 July 1966, p. 10. See also Albert Ramalingam, Oil probe: Jap firm to spend millions in *The Straits Times*, 4 February 1969, p. 5. See also Anonymous, Japanese to spend $10m in oil probe off Sabah in *The Straits Times*, 20 July 1970, p. 5.

[54] Anonymous, French, Japanese combine to start oil hunt in *The Straits Times*, 8 May 1969, p. 6. See also Anonymous, Sabah projects in *The Straits Times*, 3 December 1969, p. 23.

[55] Anonymous, Japanese to spend US$ssom to exploit Sabah copper in *The Straits Times*, 31 May 1969, p. 6. See also Anonymous, Japan gets license to prospect in *The Straits Times*, 10 December 1967, p. 11. See also Anonymous, Firm to begin copper mining in Sabah in *The Straits Times*, 8 July 1968, p. 7. See also Anonymous, Move to resume Sabah copper mine project in *New Nation*, 26 October 1972, p. 7. See also Anonymous, JAPANESE TO INVEST IN $260M SABAH COPPER VENTURE in *The Straits Times*, 20 February 1973, p. 22. See also Anonymous, JAPAN OFFERS AID FOR SABAH COPPER in *The Straits*

mangrove wood factory in Sabah in November 1971,[56] Overseas Mineral Resources Development Co. and Mamut Mines Development plan to begin full-scale production of copper ore from the Mamut mine in April 1973.[57]

Conclusion

Japan is willing to provide technical assistance to North Borneo to help its development under the Colombo Plan, especially in agriculture and fisheries. There is interest from Japanese entrepreneurs to invest in Sabah. They are interested in agricultural development and exploitation of Sabah mineral resources. Japanese entrepreneurs that come are encouraged to form a joint venture with local capital. Japanese interest in Sabah economic development after the formation of Malaysia can be seen through donations, official visits, economic visits and social visits from time to time. There is also the entry of Japanese investments from time to time.

Reference

Albert Ramalingam. 1967. Firm offers 50 youths training with pay in Japan. *The Straits Times*, 22 March: 6.

Albert Ramalingam. 1969. Oil probe: Jap firm to spend millions. *The Straits Times*, 4 February: 5.

Anonymous. 1894. JAPANESE IMMIGRATION IN BRITISH NORTH BORNEO. *The Straits Times*, 31 May: 24.

Anonymous. 1895. JAPANESE IN BRITISH NORTH BORNEO. *The Straits Times*, 21 January: 3.

Anonymous. 1949. 5 MILLION IMPORTS FROM JAPAN. *The Straits Times*, 16 November: 1.

Anonymous. 1950. $1mil. Import From Japan. *The Straits Times*, 31 March: 4.

Times, 16 August 1966, p. 7. See also A. Ramalingam, Japanese firm to prospect for copper in Sabah in *The Straits Times*, 13 March 1968, p. 6.

[56] Anonymous, Kilang kayu bakau keluar hasil akhir bulan ini in *Berita Harian*, 8 November 1971, p. 11.

[57] Mok Sin Pin, $80m project to produce copper in Sabah in *The Straits Times*, 2 April 1973, p. 16.

Anonymous. 1950. Awards May Be Paid This Year. NORTH BORNEO WAR DAMAGE. *The Straits Times*, 28 April: 4.

Anonymous. 1952. Japs want to develop North Borneo. *The Singapore Free Press*, 23 July: 3.

Anonymous. 1957. Trade boost plan. *The Straits Times*, 31 March: 11.

Anonymous. 1957. Japan pledges support for North Borneo. OFFER TO HELP AGRICULTURE, FISHERIES... *The Straits Times*, 9 April: 12.

Anonymous. 1959. Japanese industry team for Borneo. *The Straits Times*, 18 April: 2.

Anonymous. 1959. Jepun na' lawat Borneo Utara. *Berita Harian*, 2 May: 3.

Anonymous. 1960. JAPAN'S RUBBER IMPORTS FALL OFF. *The Straits Times*, 1 January: 12.

Anonymous. 1960. Japan rubber imports up. *The Straits Times*, 12 January: 10.

Anonymous. 1961. Diplomats tour N. Borneo. *The Straits Times*, 8 March: 16.

Anonymous. 1961. North Borneo bid for investment cash from abroad. NEEDED TO HELP SPEED THE TERRITORY'S TRADE AND INDUSTRIAL DEVELOPMENT. *The Straits Times*, 1 December: 13.

Anonymous. 1963. Borneo timber is one of territories' big exports to Japan. TRADE WITH BORNEO. *The Straits Times*, 15 September: 1.

Anonymous. 1963. Japan's technical co-operation. *The Straits Times*, 15 September: 7.

Anonymous. 1964. Japan offers five scholarships. *The Straits Times*, 4 April: 6.

Anonymous. 1964. Japan to have man in Borneo. *The Straits Times*, 15 May: 8.

Anonymous. 1964. New fishing firm in Sandakan. *The Straits Times*, 24 May: 10.

Anonymous. 1964. Japan keen to take part in Sabah development. *The Straits Times*, 30 May: 9.

Anonymous. 1964. JAPANESE INTEREST IN SABAH PROJECTS. *The Straits Times*, 5 October: 11.

Anonymous. 1964. JAPANESE AWARDS FOR SABAH, SARAWAK. *The Straits Times*, 11 December: 11.

Anonymous. 1965. 7 Japanese peace corps volunteers due. *The Straits Times*, 24 December: 11.

Anonymous. 1965. Minyak di-Sabah. 'Kemungkinan baik': Empat sharikat asing di-beri lesen. *Berita Harian*, 28 December: 1.

Anonymous. 1966. JAPANESE TO DRILL OIL WELLS IN BORNEO. *The Straits Times*, 5 July: 10.

Anonymous. 1966. JAPAN OFFERS AID FOR SABAH COPPER. *The Straits Times*, 16 August: 7.

Anonymous. 1966. Tokyo offers Sabah two scholarships. *The Straits Times*, 25 September: 14.

Anonymous. 1966. Lo: Japanese keen to invest in Sabah. *The Straits Times*, 29 November: 13.

Anonymous. 1967. 6 NEGARA AKAN MELIHAT P-RAYA SABAH. *Berita Harian*, 22 March: 1.

Anonymous. 1967. JEPUN KIRIM PEMERHATI2 KA-PILEHAN RAYA SABAH. *Berita Harian*, 31 March: 3.

Anonymous. 1967. Sharikat Jepun di-beri hak korek tembaga. Bakal lombong paling besar di-Malaysia. *Berita Harian*, 17 November: 1.

Anonymous. 1967. Japan gets license to prospect. *The Straits Times*, 10 December: 11.

Anonymous. 1967. Jepun mula buat jalan menuju lombong tembaga. *Berita Harian*, 28 December: 3.

Anonymous. 1968. Firm to begin copper mining in Sabah. *The Straits Times*, 8 July: 7.

Anonymous. 1968. Sukarelawan Jepun. *Berita Harian*, 8 December: 12.

Anonymous. 1969. Sharikat dari Jepun di-berikan tugas. BERJUTA2 UNTOK MENCHARI MINYAK. *Berita Harian*, 4 February: 2.

Anonymous. 1969. French, Japanese combine to start oil hunt. *The Straits Times*, 8 May: 6.

Anonymous. 1969. Japanese to spend USssom to exploit Sabah copper. *The Straits Times*, 31 May: 6.

Anonymous. 1969. $200,000 untok Expo dari Sabah. *Berita Harian*, 7 August: 1.

Anonymous. 1969. Sabah projects. *The Straits Times*, 3 December: 23.

Anonymous. 1970. 10 volunteers from Japan. *The Straits Times*, 7 April: 15.

Anonymous. 1970. Sabah bananas for Japan. *The Straits Times*, 11 May: 6.

Anonymous. 1970. Sharikat2 chari emas dan Perak di-Sabah. *Berita Harian*, 12 May: 3.

Anonymous. 1970. Japanese to spend $10m in oil probe off Sabah. *The Straits Times*, 20 July: 5.

Anonymous. 1971. Kilang kayu bakau keluar hasil akhir bulan ini. *Berita Harian*, 8 November: 11.

Anonymous. 1972. Move to resume Sabah copper mine project. *New Nation*, 26 October: 7.

Anonymous. 1973. JAPANESE TO INVEST IN $260M SABAH COPPER VENTURE. *The Straits Times*, 20 February: 22.

Anonymous. 1978. Nippon Koei to oversee Sabah power project. *The Business Times*, 9 September: 2.

Anonymous. 1979. Hydro-power contract. *The Straits Times*, 1 March: 13.

Anonymous. 1979. Joint timber office in Tokyo. *The Business Times*, 31 May: 3.

Anonymous. 1981. Marubeni in Sabah veneer venture. *The Business Times*, 8 July: 2.

Anonymous. 1981. Sabah cocoa venture. *The Straits Times*, 4 November: 19.

Anonymous. 1982. JAPAN IS URGED TO OFFER HELP TO SABAH. *The Straits Times*, 10 February: 13.

Anonymous. 1984. Sabah gets $2 m 'peace garden' from Japan. *The Straits Times*, 17 April: 15.

Anonymous. 1984. Japanese gift of $15,000 to ape centre. *The Straits Times*, 9 June: 20.

Anonymous. 1988. Menlu belum lihat filem. *Berita Harian*, 20 June: 2.

Anonymous. 1994. Invest in east coast, Sabah and Sarawak: Mahathir. *The Straits Times*, 28 July: 15.

A. Ramalingam. 1968. Japanese firm to prospect for copper in Sabah. *The Straits Times*, 13 March: 6.

Chee Peng Lim & Lee Poh Ping. 1979. *The Role of Japanese Direct Investment in Malaysia*. Occasional Paper No. 60. Singapore: Institute of Southeast Asian Studies.

Chee Peng Lim & Lee Poh Ping. 1983. Japanese Direct Investment in Malaysia, with Special Reference to Japanese Joint Ventures. In Sueo Sekiguchi (editor). *ASEAN-Japan Relations Investment*, pp. 61-92. Singapore: Institute of Southeast Asian Studies.

James Chia. 1968. Sabah: Jepun meluaskan rancangan ekonomi-nya. *Berita Harian*, 16 September: 3.

Makoto Anazawa. 1994. Japanese Manufacturing Investment in Malaysia. In Jomo, K.S. (editor). *Japan and Malaysian Development: In the shadow of the rising sun*, pp. 75-101. London: Routledge.

Md. Ali Hasan. 1996. *Pelaburan Langsung Jepun di* Malaysia. Kertas kerja Kongres Sejarah Malaysia II - Sejarah dan Proses Pemantapan Negara Bangsa. Anjuran Persatuan Sejarah Malaysia dengan kerjasama Jabatan Sejarah UKM. Bilik Jumaah UKM, Bangi, 26-28 November.

Md. Saffie bin Abdul Rahim. 2005. *Sejarah Kegiatan Ekonomi Orang Jepun di Borneo Utara sebelum Perang Dunia Kedua (1890-1941)*. Master's Thesis in Literature. Sekolah Sains Sosial, Universiti Malaysia Sabah.

Md. Saffie Abdul Rahim. 2007. *Jepun di Borneo Utara: Migrasi dan Kegiatan Ekonomi 1884-1941*. Kota Kinabalu: Penerbit UMS.

Mehmet Sami Denker. 1990. *Internationalization of the Malaysian Economy: Role of Japan*. Ph.D. Thesis. Universiti Malaya.

Mehmet Sami Denker. 1994. The Evolution of Japanese Investment in Malaysia. In Jomo, K.S. (editor). *Japan and Malaysian Development: In the shadow of the rising sun*, pp. 44-74. London: Routledge.

Mok Sin Pin. 1973. $80m project to produce copper in Sabah. *The Straits Times*, 2 April: 16.

Sabihah Osman. 1998. Japanese economic activities in North Borneo from the 1890s until 1941. *Journal of Southeast Asian Studies* 29 (1): 24-43.

Yutaka Shimomoto & Mandalam, K. Ravi (editors). 2010. *Japanese Immigrants and Investments in North Borneo*. Kota Kinabalu: The Sabah Society.